RUGBY
THE INTERNATIONAL GAME

A PHOTOGRAPHIC CELEBRATION BY

COLIN WHELAN

TEXT BY PAT BOOTH
FOREWORD BY IAN McGEECHAN

Queen Anne Press

A Queen Anne Press Book

Queen Anne Press is
a division of
Lennard Associates Limited
Mackerye End, Harpenden
Hertfordshire AL5 5DR

Rugby - The International Game
was first published in New Zealand in 1994 by
Moa Beckett in association with
Action Photographics (Aust)

© Action Photographics (Aust) Pty. Limited
& Moa Beckett Publishers Limited

ISBN 1-85291-554-4

Designed by Suellen Allen

Typeset by Typeset Graphics, Auckland

Printed through Bookbuilders, Hong Kong

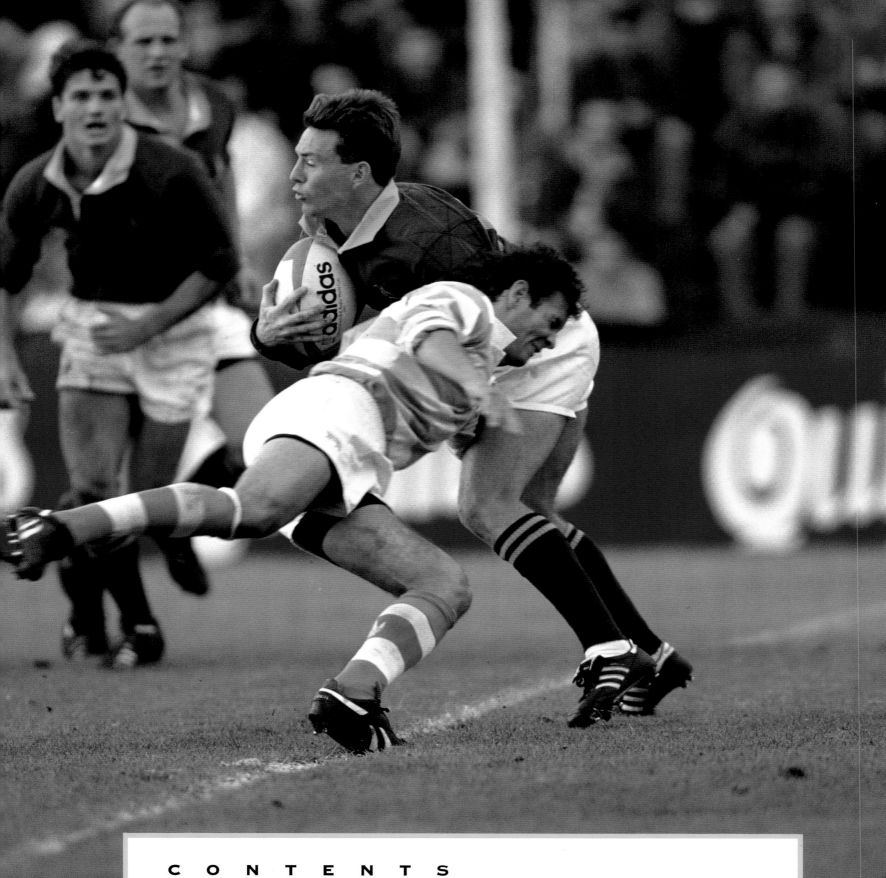

C O N T E N T S

F O R E W O R D

RUGBY IS A GAME OF SPEED, SKILL AND PHYSICAL
AGGRESSION, AND THE CLOSER YOU GET TO THE ACTION THE
MORE IMPRESSIVE IT LOOKS. WITHOUT ACTUALLY PARTICIPATING,
ONLY THE CAMERA CAN CONVEY THIS AWESOME INVOLVEMENT.
WHAT THIS BOOK BRINGS TO US IS THAT UNIQUE EXPERIENCE,
WITH THE OUTSTANDING PHOTOGRAPHY OF COLIN WHELAN
ENCAPSULATING THE ESSENCE OF RUGBY AT THE HIGHEST LEVEL
FROM THE NORTHERN AND SOUTHERN HEMISPHERES. THESE
PHOTOGRAPHS DESCRIBE THE GAME EVEN MORE GRAPHICALLY
THAN THE THOUSANDS OF WORDS WRITTEN THROUGHOUT EACH
SEASON; THEY EXCITE AND EVOKE A RESPONSE, AS WELL AS
REVIVING MEMORIES OF GAMES SEEN, OR FOLLOWED THROUGH A
NEWSPAPER REPORT.

THE SHEER QUALITY OF PRESENTATION, ALLIED TO THE SKILL OF
THE PHOTOGRAPHER, GIVES US AN ALMOST LIVING REMINDER OF A
GAME THAT IS NOW PLAYED THROUGHOUT THE WORLD. WHEN THE
ACTUAL OCCASIONS FEATURED ARE LONG FORGOTTEN, THE IMPACT
OF THESE IMAGES WILL REMAIN, COVERING ALL FACETS OF THE
GAME, FROM ITS COMPETITIVENESS TO ITS FRIENDSHIPS, FROM THE
BUILD-UP TO THE FINAL WHISTLE AND BEYOND.

IAN MCGEECHAN
JUNE 1994

I N T R O D U C T I O N

To the historian, test rugby is points tallied, matches won, rubbers squared and lost, records broken. Comparisons, statistics and team lists.

To the players, it is tries scored, penalties kicked and missed, team triumphs and disasters, personal milestones and nightmares. What was and what might have been — what should have been, what will be next time.

For spectators, matches are in sharp focus — points for and against, results and why. The nervous tension of the build-up, the excitement of the event and then the seemingly endless post-mortems to follow.

But international rugby is much more than any or all of these things — it is faces and places, hope, exhilaration and despair, ambitions and lost opportunities, skills and tactics, instinct and deliberate decision, events and reactions, results and aftermaths.

And pride.

Someone once wrote: "Fame is the spur." In international rugby, the word is pride.
It spurs individuals and teams, raising determination and skill levels, making good players great, determined players apparently invincible, drawing on often unrecognised reserves and fitness.

This is test rugby.

It is a customs officer from Marseilles leaving behind his files and flying to Paris and a sporting call to arms, a physical education instructor from Devon packing his tracksuit and heading for Twickenham, a novice marketing manager from Brisbane getting an early plane to Sydney, a farmer from Kaeo for the first time in the unfamiliar dressing rooms at Eden Park, a winger from a Samoan village half the world away feeling the history of Cardiff Arms Park, a student from Kyoto like a modern samurai facing the drama of an All Black haka, a nervous policeman from Budapest in the stand tunnel at Dublin.

It is the atmosphere on the bus to the ground, the glimpses of eager faces on the streets, the quiet determination of those around you.

It is pre-match nerves under the stand — colour and noise above.

It is scarves and flags, banners and slogans in the high-terraced seating, knitted hats and pies, takeaways from caravans and champagne in the boots of Rolls Royces, home-made sandwiches eaten in seats won at a club raffle.

It is bands, short-skirted cheerleaders, the chorus of boot studs on the

BARE FLOOR OF THE CHANGING ROOM, THE QUIET TALK OF OLD MEN WITH LONG MEMORIES IN THE SEATS OF HONOUR ABOVE.

THEY HAVE BEEN THERE BEFORE YOU. THEY HAVE KNOWN IT, FELT IT. NOW THEY REMEMBER AND THEY FEEL FOR YOU.

IT IS THE NEVER-CHANGING EMOTION OF PULLING ON THAT REVERED JERSEY FOR THE FIRST OR THE FIFTIETH TIME, OF HEARING YOUR NATIONAL ANTHEM PLAYED, THE ROAR OF THE CROWD, THE HIGH FIVES OF YOUR TEAM-MATES. SWEATY ARMS AROUND YOU AT THE FINAL WHISTLE.

IT IS THE JOY OF HOME FANS RUSHING THEIR HEROES.

IT IS THE GREEN GRASS WITH A COVER OF SNOW AT MURRAYFIELD, A SURFACE LIKE ROCK AT PORT ELIZABETH, MUD TO THE ANKLES AT LANCASTER PARK, THE BITTER COLD OF AN ATHLETIC PARK SOUTHERLY, THE THIN AIR OF THE HIGH VELDT, GLARING TROPICAL SUN AT SUVA, THE WINTER NIGHT CLOSING IN AROUND PARIS.

IT IS TENSION ON THE FACE OF A SELECTOR SMOKING A CIGAR BEHIND THE GOALPOSTS IN WELLINGTON, OR ANOTHER LEANING FORWARD IN A BID TO GET CLOSER TO THE PLAY AT LA BEAUJOIRE STADIUM, AT FERROCARRIL OR ELLIS PARK.

IT IS FATHERS, MOTHERS, WIVES, GIRLFRIENDS, WORKMATES, KNOWING WHAT HAS GONE BEFORE AND WILLING EVENTS TO COME.

IT IS PEOPLE SAYING "IT'S ONLY A GAME" WHILE YOU AND THEY KNOW DEEP DOWN THAT IT IS SO MUCH MORE THAN THAT.

IT IS A SERIES OF CONTESTS, MAN AGAINST MAN, TEAM AGAINST TEAM, STYLE AGAINST STYLE, A STRUGGLE AGAINST ERROR AND MISJUDGEMENT, AGAINST LAPSES OF CONCENTRATION AND OF SKILL, ONLY MOMENTARY IN TERMS OF TIME — BUT CRUCIAL IN A MATCH, IN A SEASON, IN A CAREER.

MOMENTS, EVEN SECONDS, WHEN POINTS ARE SCORED, WHEN REPUTATIONS ARE WON AND LOST.

IT IS THE DOUBLE DEMAND OF WANTING TO SUCCEED AND DREADING FAILURE.

IT IS POWER. PHYSICAL POWER, THE STRENGTH TO DOMINATE IN SCRUM AND LINE-OUT, THE MENTAL POWER TO ABSORB TACTICS AND TO VARY THEM AS THE ROLLER-COASTER PATTERN OF A MATCH UNFOLDS.

THE POWER OF PURPOSE AND PRIDE . . .

IT IS INSTANTS WHICH FLASH AND EXPLODE WITH FLAIR, WITH THE UNEXPECTED, THE UNMATCHABLE, WHEN REFLEXES TAKE OVER, TECHNIQUE AND CONDITIONING ARE GIVEN NEW THRUST, MATCH-SHAPING PURPOSE AND PERFORMANCE.

IT IS THE INDIVIDUAL SPEED OF PLAYERS, THE COMBINED SPEED OF TEAMS, THE TOTAL PACE OF ATTACK AND DEFENCE, THRUST AND COUNTER-THRUST WHICH CHALLENGES THOSE WHO PLAY AND GRIPS THOSE WHO WATCH.

IT IS SPEED OF MIND, OF DECISION AND OF MOVEMENT.

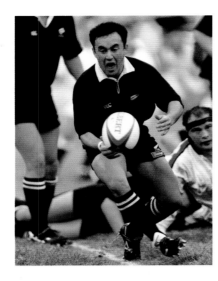

IT IS THE COURAGE OF THOSE WHO ARE PUT TO THE TEST, WHO REFUSE TO BOW TO THE ODDS, NO MATTER HOW SEVERE, WHO NEVER LOSE THEIR DETERMINATION TO WIN, WHO HAVE STRENGTH OF MIND AND BODY TO COME BACK WHEN EVERYTHING SEEMS LOST, WHEN THE TOUGHEST OPPONENT OF ALL SEEMS TO BE THE CLOCK BESIDE THE SCOREBOARD.

IT IS PAIN TOO, AGONY FROM INJURIES WHICH TEMPORARILY OR PERMANENTLY STRIP CHAMPIONS OF THEIR TALENT, WHICH UNEXPECTEDLY DICTATE EVENTS, PUTTING NEW DEMANDS ON INDIVIDUALS AND TEAMS.

IT IS THE EMOTIONAL PAIN OF DISAPPOINTMENT, THE NUMBING ACHE OF LOSS AND PERCEIVED FAILURE.

IT IS THE COLD BITE OF RAIN AND WIND FOR MEN WHO PLANNED FOR WARM SUNSHINE AND A SMOOTH TURF, FOR A GOOD FOOTING, AND WHO GOT NONE OF THESE THINGS.

IT IS MORE OFTEN, THOUGH, THE MEMORIES WHICH ARE THE JOYS OF THE GAME, OF SKILLS AT A PEAK, OF PERFORMANCES AND POINTS, SHARED VICTORIES AND PERSONAL TRIUMPHS.

IT IS THE NOISE OF THE CROWD, A SPONTANEOUS MEXICAN WAVE, THE SOUND OF *LAND OF OUR FATHERS,* A SAMOAN WAR DANCE, SILENCE AS THE KICKER STEADIES HIMSELF WITH FULL TIME ON THE CLOCK.

IT IS THE CHOSEN LONELINESS OF THE REFEREE, THE EMPTINESS OF THE GROUND IN THE DUSK AFTERWARDS, THE SCOREBOARD TELLING ITS SIMPLISTIC STORY OF THE MATCH AS THE STATISTICIANS SAW IT.

IT IS, FOR PLAYERS THEN, SHARED EXHAUSTION AND PLEASURE, SOMETIMES BOISTEROUS, SOMETIMES QUIET. SOME STILL IN JERSEYS AND BOOTS, SOME WITH EXCHANGED FOREIGN JERSEYS SLUNG AROUND THEIR SHOULDERS, SAVOURING THE MOMENT, DRINKS IN HAND, SINGING, LAUGHING ABOVE THE POP OF CORKS AND THE CLICKS OF OPENING CANS.

OR IN THE STEAMY BATH AND SHOWER ROOM, RIDDING THEMSELVES OF THE MUD, THE ACHES AND THE STRAINS – BUT NOT THE JOY OF IT ALL.

FOR SOME, THE DRESSING ROOMS ARE QUIET AND FILLED WITH REGRET AND THE SOFT WORDS OF WELL-WISHERS. NOT EVERYONE CAN WIN.

THERE IS A FEELING IN THOSE PLACES OF STRONG WORDS TO COME, A LINGERING DREAD ABOUT THE NEXT TEAM TALK, OF PERHAPS BEING THERE AND BEING PART OF IT ALL FOR THE LAST TIME, OF SHARING RESPONSIBILITY, AND EVEN BLAME. OF CHANCES LOST AS WELL AS MATCHES.

THE LANGUAGE AND THE PLACE DO NOT MATTER.

IT IS INTERNATIONAL RUGBY AT CARDIFF ARMS OR CARISBROOK, NEWLANDS OR NAGOYA, TWICKENHAM OR TOULOUSE, BALLYMORE OR BUENOS AIRES, MILAN OR MELBOURNE.

IT IS A BALLBOY WITH THE BALL SO RECENTLY HANDLED BY HIS HEROES, HIS PALMS PRESSED AGAINST IT, DREAMING HIS DREAMS.

PART 1

OFF
THE
FIELD

ANYWHERE, ANY TIME, NO
MATTER WHAT THE
DISCOMFORT. AS LONG AS YOU
ARE THERE!

MESH AND WIRE FOR A SPORT

WHICH. BY 1994. IN FACT

KNOWS NO BARRIERS.

COME RAIN, COME HEAT, COME

HAIL, COME SNOW, COME

VICTORY, COME DEFEAT,

THEY'LL STILL COME.

PATRIOTISM AND PAINT — NEW
MEANING TO AN OLD TRUTH
ABOUT EMOTION (AND
LOYALTY) BEING WRITTEN ON
THEIR FACES.

THERE'LL BE A TIME, DECADES
FROM NOW, WHEN HE'LL BE
PROUD TO HAVE BEEN THERE.
NO NEED THEN TO MAKE UP
MEMORIES. THIS PHOTO WILL
BE HIS PROOF.

NEVER ANY DOUBT WHO THEIR
CHEERS ARE FOR. THEY WEAR
THEIR ALLEGIANCE ON THEIR
CHESTS AND CARRY IT ON
THEIR VOICES TOO.

SCARVES GALORE, NATIONAL

SONGS AND FILLED ROLLS

FOR EVERYONE — LOYALTY

NEEDS FEEDING.

TWO VERSIONS OF NAME
DROPPING – IT'S ALL PART OF
THE PRE-GAME RITUALS,
SIMPLY FILLING IN TIME
UNTIL KICK-OFF.

27

PUSHING UP THE CROWD'S

EXPECTATIONS BEFORE THE

MAIN EVENT.

DAY OR NIGHT, UNDER THE

MOUNTAINS, HIGH ON THE

VELDT, IN THE SNOW OF

SCOTLAND, IN THE HEAT OF

AUSTRALIA . . .

ON THE LINE AND LAYING IT ON THE LINE. WITH THE RULEBOOK IN THEIR MINDS AND THE WHISTLE IN THEIR HANDS THEY TELL IT THE WAY IT IS GOING TO BE . . . WHILE POLICE FACE THE POSSIBILITY OF TROUBLE.

SO CLOSE TO THE ACTION AND
YET SO FAR, FEELING THE
TENSION, SHARING THE PAIN,
WILLING THEMSELVES INTO A
PLACE WITHOUT WISHING
TEAM-MATES HARM.

THE LONG HOURS UNDER

FLOODLIGHTS ARE OVER. THE

TEAM TALKS ENDED. THE

TACTICS DECIDED. THE ADVICE

GIVEN. NOW THE COACHES ARE

MEN ALONE . . .

FINAL WHISTLE AND THE POST-
MORTEMS ARE STILL A FEW
HOURS AWAY. FOR NOW, IT'S A
PAT ON THE BACK, SYMPATHY
AND QUIET WORDS.

TIRED MUSCLES, CRAMP AND
STRAIN, FEELING THE
PRESSURE. WILL THEY LAST
THE DISTANCE AT THE
HIGHEST LEVEL?

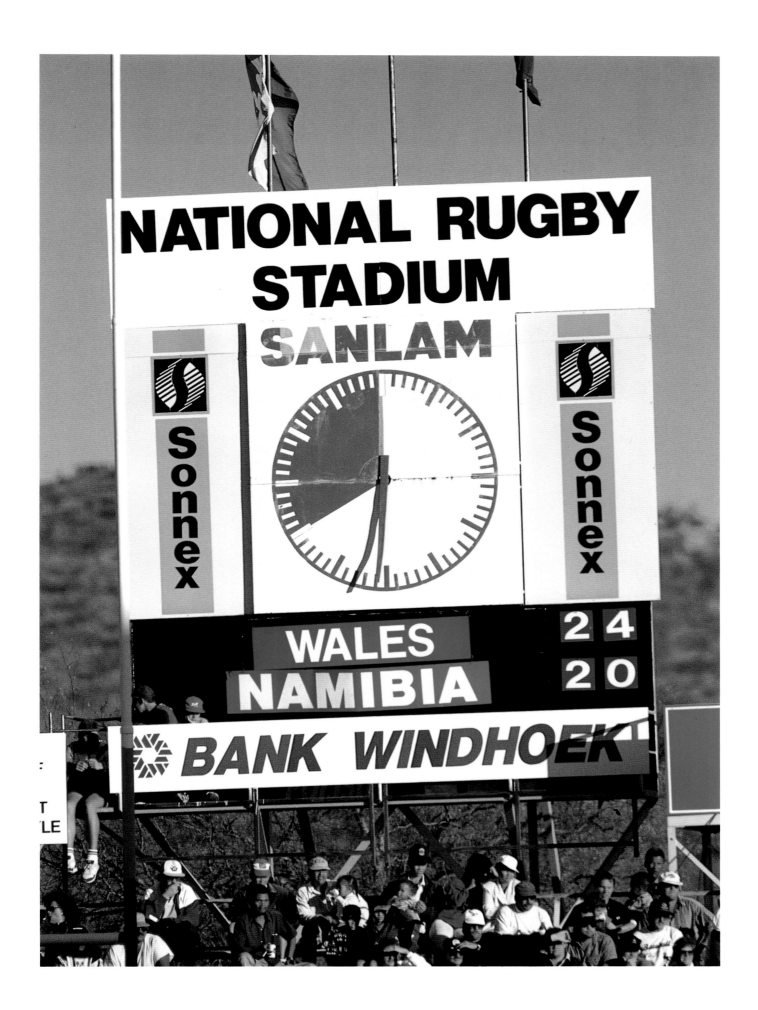

AFTER THE MATCH, A SECOND

TEST — BY MEDIA. LIKE THE

PLAYERS, THEY ARE

SOMETIMES GOOD, SOMETIMES

BAD, SOMETIMES CLUMSY,

SOMETIMES CLEVER,

SOMETIMES INCISIVE,

SOMETIMES BRUTAL. BUT

ALWAYS THERE.

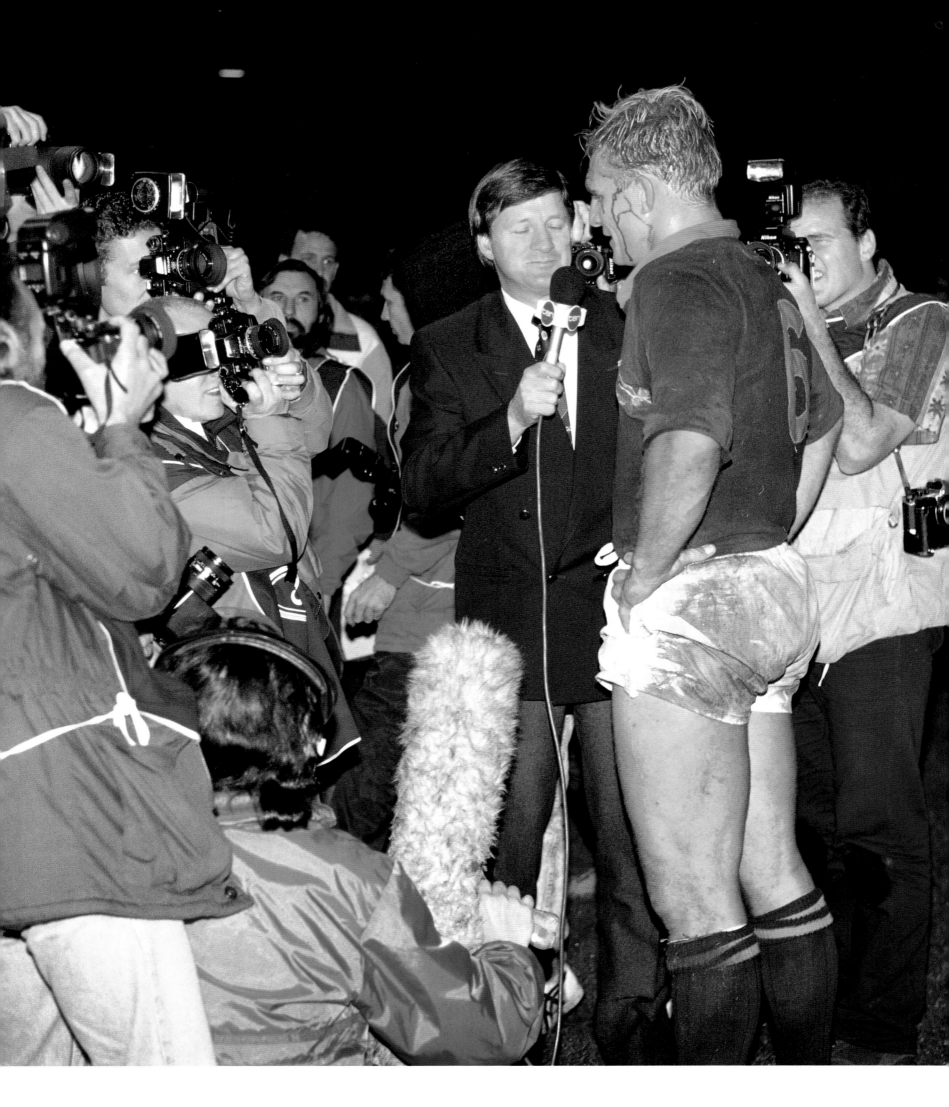

O N
T H E
F I E L D

PRIDE

'IN RUGBY, THE WORD
IS PRIDE. IT GRIPS
PEOPLE, COMMUNITIES
AND COUNTRIES, MAKES
GOOD PLAYERS GREAT,
DETERMINED PLAYERS
APPARENTLY INVINCIBLE'

SHOULDER TO SHOULDER AS

THE ANTHEM IS PLAYED,

HEARING THE SOUND OF

SINGING AND FEELING A

ONENESS WITH EACH OTHER

AND WITH THE VOICES IN THE

HIGH STANDS AROUND THEM.

THE ALL BLACK HAKA — A
CHALLENGE TO THEIR
OPPONENTS AND TO
THEMSELVES, THEIR SKILLS
AND THEIR COURAGE.

THOSE MOMENTS WHEN 15 MEN

BECOME A TEAM, LINKED BY

PATRIOTISM AND PURPOSE.

THE TRICOLOUR AND THE

MARSEILLAISE — THE EPITOME

OF PRIDE AND OF PURPOSE.

CONTEST

'MAN AGAINST MAN,
TEAM AGAINST TEAM,
STYLE AGAINST STYLE,
MOMENTS WHEN
MATCHES AND
REPUTATIONS ARE WON
AND LOST'

SOMETIMES, IT IS MAN TO MAN

IN THE VERY REAL MEANING OF

THE WORDS — EYEBALL TO

EYEBALL, WILL TO WILL.

STRENGTH OF BODY AND
STRENGTH OF WILL IN THE
BATTLE FOR POSSESSION –
WHERE FITNESS AND COURAGE
ARE THE ESSENTIALS, WHERE
TESTS ARE WON AND LOST.

IN THE SPLIT-SECOND, HIGH-
ALTITUDE CHALLENGE OF THE
LINEOUT, WHERE THE BATTLE
IS AGAINST THE LAW OF
GRAVITY AS WELL AS YOUR
OPPONENT, SKILL AND
TECHNIQUE ARE PARAMOUNT,
ALONG WITH TIMING,
TEAMWORK — AND A LITTLE
HELP FROM YOUR FRIENDS!

STRENGTH

'STRENGTH TO
DOMINATE, MENTAL
POWER TO ABSORB
TACTICS AND TO VARY
THEM, THE POWER OF
PURPOSE'

THAT BLEND OF BALANCE,
DETERMINATION AND POWER
WHICH LIFTS A PLAYER AND A
TEAM FROM THE ORDINARY,
THAT MOMENT IN A MATCH
WHEN A DEFENCE IS PUT TO
THE ULTIMATE TEST.

AN IMPRESSION OF

INEVITABILITY, COMBINING

OPPORTUNITY AND

DETERMINATION, BREAKING

THE POWER AND CONTROL OF
THE FORWARDS HAS DONE ITS
JOB, A QUICK GLANCE, AN
EVEN QUICKER PASS AND THE
BACKS WILL BE RUNNING FREE.

AS IF THEY WERE BRED FOR

THEIR ROLE, SOME PLAYERS

SEEM TO HAVE THOSE INBORN

QUALITIES OF STRENGTH AND

DETERMINATION WHICH TEST

MATCHES DEMAND OF THOSE

WHO PLAY IN THEM.

PACE

'THRUST AND
COUNTER-THRUST . . .
SPEED OF MIND,
DECISION AND
MOVEMENT'

THE BALL IN HAND, A GAP IN

HIS SIGHTS AND SUPPORT AT

HAND — ONE OF THOSE

COMBINATIONS WHICH TURN A

MATCH AND SOMETIMES MAKE A

CAREER.

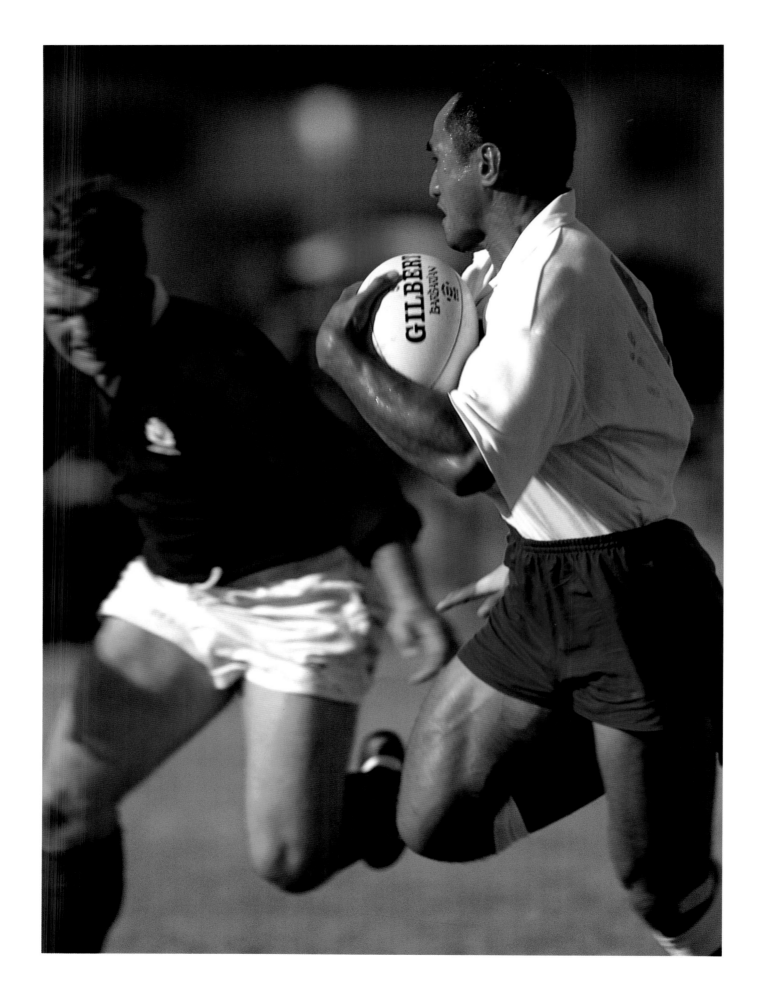

ON THE BREAK AND ON THE
MOVE — ALL EYES ON THE
ATTACKER, THE DEFENCE AND
THE HIGH BALL.

FLAIR

'THE UNMATCHABLE,
THE UNEXPECTED,
WHEN REFLEXES TAKE
OVER, MOMENTS WHICH
FLASH AND EXPLODE'

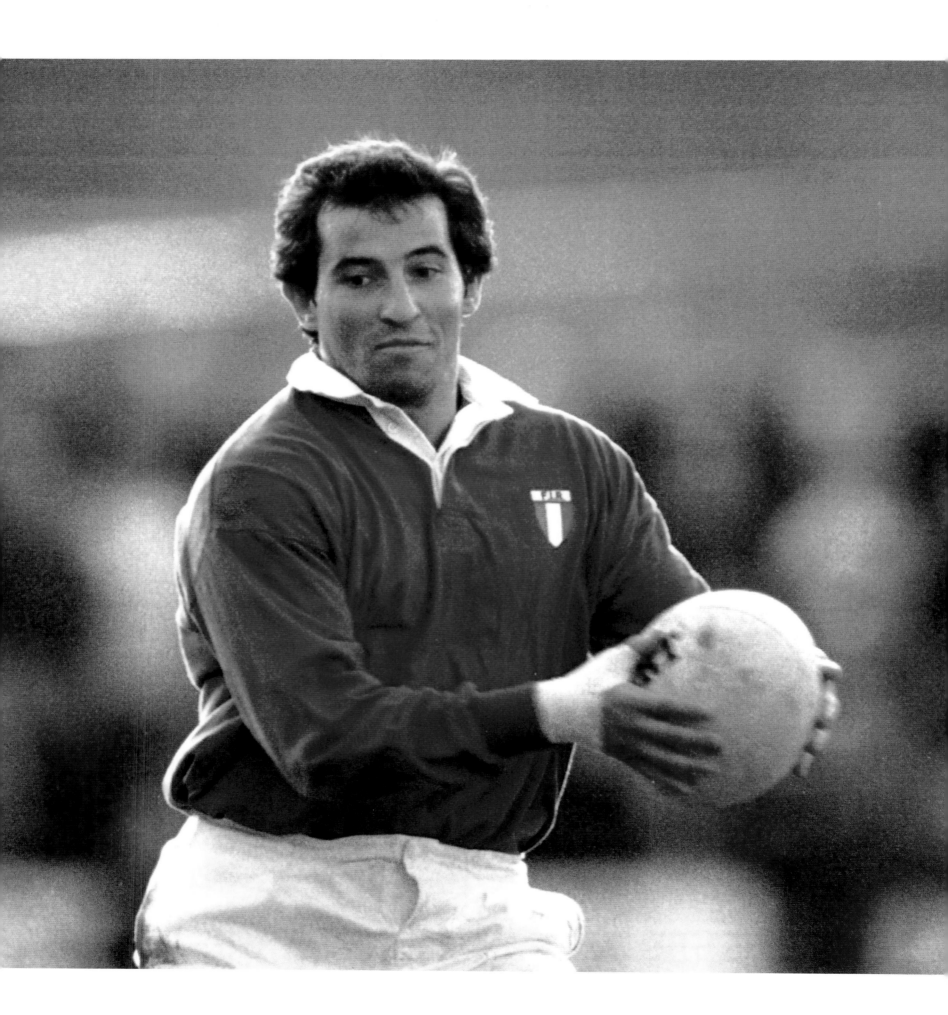

OFF HIS FEET AND THE BALL

ON ITS WAY, ONE MAN'S

INSTINCTIVE TRIBUTE TO THE

GREAT DANIE CRAVEN, SAID TO

HAVE INVENTED THE DIVE PASS

JUST FOR MOMENTS LIKE THIS.

OFF HIS FEET AND THE BALL
ON ITS WAY, ONE MAN'S
INSTINCTIVE TRIBUTE TO THE
GREAT DANIE CRAVEN, SAID TO
HAVE INVENTED THE DIVE PASS
JUST FOR MOMENTS LIKE THIS.

NO RISK TOO GREAT, NO

EFFORT TOO MUCH — TOTAL

COMMITMENT IN AN AERIAL

CLASH FOR THE BALL, THE

SORT OF INVOLVEMENT A TEST

DEMANDS AND GETS.

COURAGE

'INDEFINABLE
PERSONAL STRENGTHS
ARE PUT TO THE REAL
TEST, FOR THOSE WHO
REFUSE TO BOW TO THE
ODDS, WHO COME BACK
WHEN EVERYTHING
SEEMS LOST'

BANDAGES AND BLOCKBUSTING

ATTACK AS THE DEFENCE HAS

REAL PRESSURE ON IT.

POSSESSION – GAINING IT,
RETAINING IT AND HANDING IT
ON – KEY TO INTERNATIONAL
SUCCESS AND THE PRODUCT
OF TOTAL PERSONAL
INVOLVEMENT.

THE VITAL FACTOR IS
DETERMINATION PLUS AN
ABSOLUTE AND PERSONAL
PROMISE TO GIVE EVERYTHING
IN THE CAUSE, REGARDLESS OF
THE CHALLENGE, EVEN IF — AS
HALFBACK — YOU ARE THE
SMALLEST PLAYER ON THE
FIELD.

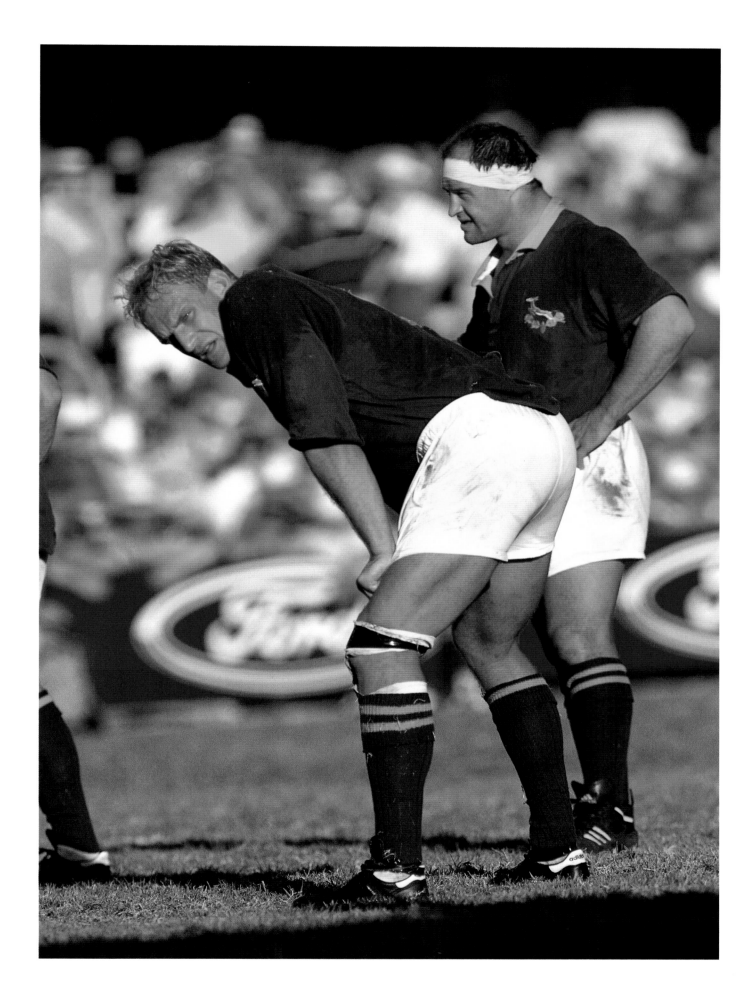

PAIN

'THE AGONY OF
INJURIES STRIPS
CHAMPIONS OF THEIR
TALENTS AND OTHERS
OF THEIR
OPPORTUNITIES . . .
THE PAIN OF
DISAPPOINTMENT AND
OF PERCEIVED LOSS'

TO THE SIDELINE,

UNWILLINGLY, WITH THE

DEFINITE FEELING THAT, GIVEN

HALF A CHANCE, HE WILL BE

BACK.

ONE MAN IN HIS PERSONAL
PAIN. TWO THOUGHTS IN HIS
MIND: HOW SERIOUS IS THE
INJURY, AND HOW LONG
BEFORE HE CAN RE-TAKE HIS
PLACE?

THOUSANDS WATCH AND WILL

HIM BACK. NO ONE WISHES HIM

BACK MORE THAN HE HIMSELF.

DEEP IN HIS BLANKETS AND

HIS DESPAIR AS THE ACTION

HE WAS SO RECENTLY PART OF

GOES ON A FEW METRES AWAY.

HE CAN HEAR IT, SENSE IT,

BUT CANNOT BEAR TO WATCH.

JOY

'THE SHARED
VICTORIES AND
PERSONAL TRIUMPHS
. . . THESE ARE
THE TIMES TO
REMEMBER'

THE TRY SCORED, THE MATCH

PATTERN CHANGED, SHARED

PLEASURE AND ANTICIPATION.

SALUTES TO SUCCESS — THE

EMOTION LINKS THOSE WHO

WIN AND THOSE WHO WATCH.

POPPING THE CORK ON THE

JOY OF VICTORY AND

SPREADING IT AROUND.

ALL THE PREPARATIONS, ALL

THE EFFORT, ALL THE HOURS,

ALL THE SACRIFICES — IT'S

OVER AND THE WIN'S BEEN

WORTH IT.

105

CAMERADERIE

'EXHAUSTION AND
PLEASURE, SAVOURING
THE MOMENT, RIDDING
THEMSELVES OF MUD
AND SWEAT, THE ACHES
AND THE STRAINS –
BUT NOT THE PLEASURE'

JERSEYS EXCHANGED,

CONGRATULATIONS TOO, TIME

FOR OFF-THE-CUFF TOASTS TO

THE WIN AND THE WINNERS.

THESE ARE THE MOMENTS TO
REMEMBER, ONLY THE VICTORY
AND THE APPLAUSE. THE
EFFORT AND THE PAIN ARE
LEFT BEHIND. MEMORIES OF
THEM COME LATER.